MW00827840

Come Wander with Me

E. G. Chambers

Qu Chm 2/17/25

follow the Journey @ Axiom.Daze
on Instu

Come Wander with Me

Vanguard Press

VANGUARD PAPERBACK

© Copyright 2025
E. G. Chambers
art/photography created by E.G. Chambers

The right of E. G. Chambers to be identified as author of
this work has been asserted by him in accordance with the
Copyright, Designs and Patents Act 1988.

All Rights Reserved

No reproduction, copy or transmission of this publication
may be made without written permission.
No paragraph of this publication may be reproduced,
copied or transmitted save with the written permission of the
publisher, or in accordance with the provisions
of the Copyright Act 1956 (as amended).

Any person who commits any unauthorised act in relation to
this publication may be liable to criminal
prosecution and civil claims for damages.

A CIP catalogue record for this title is
available from the British Library.

ISBN 978 1 83794 059 2

Vanguard Press is an imprint of
Pegasus Elliot Mackenzie Publishers Ltd.
www.pegasuspublishers.com

First Published in 2025

Vanguard Press
Sheraton House Castle Park
Cambridge England

Printed & Bound in Great Britain

*"I dedicate this book to
my family,
my friends
and the people I met in
my 20's."*

*Among the pages in this book, "I" is not always me, "You" is not necessarily you, but "We" often refers to all of us.

Back Then

I wish I could rewrite the past,
scribbling on the pages of what used to be

though my pen bleeds invisible ink
unable to change what is set in stone,
prone in the present…
I'm lost,

like that bin of toys left in storage when we went
     elsewhere.
Sold to the highest bidder 'cause we never went back.

So much lacks substance these days.
We might as well inject
silicon in our veins,
whilst the web of devices open the gate to
our bane.

See, things were different back then, the nineties,
Socker-boppers and Saturday morning cartoons
in my 'jammies with *Captain Planet* and *The Big Comfy
     Couch*.

I wasn't privy to the deception
dealt by cruel marionettes
tugging
strings

behind the veil of society.

I wish I could give my younger self
a hug on that day our parents split up,

A fissure.
A choice.

Everything after feels like a blur,
as if the fast-forward button was
pressed on our playroom VCR.

Scenes of my life I want to remember,
but must have blocked out.

It's like the past never happened,
but then I look at my scarred
knees and remember Big Wheel races
and three sixties down our long driveway.

There were moments when I thrived as a kid,
a Rugrat on true adventures,
but now I'm all grown up,
longing for that childish bliss and curiosity.

I used to think I was invincible,
like Max Steel, the original, but I know now that
just as toys get scratched and the paint chips
with squeaky joints and coarse pivots.

We too are fated to fade with time,

the same way our
past fades in our memory.
Projected ideals in low resolution
… showing the best of us.
But I remember the worst of us too.

I know I can't change the past,
no matter how hard I try,
but wouldn't it be great if I could pop in a tape,
or stream a file, and
binge-watch a bunch of
episodes starring
the younger me.

Maybe then I'd understand
my present self better.

Pipe dreams.

Title scene.

Vivid images on a flat screen,
title reads: *Back Then*.

Twenty-One Salute

The fifth of the seventh has come and passed,
the twenty-first for me.
I have not noticed much
change,
but we do not live in third person you see.
Past events blurred to snippets; severed
parts unable to complete,
yet what has occurred still tries to compete with
the present me.
Is that why I think one way,
wish to act another day,
want,
but
cannot
find the words to say to the princess
who passes my presence,
another moment for the vault.

What is out of our control is not our fault,
yet I feel compelled to find a way to sway
society to a new motion.
Away.
So far away from its corrupt notion:
swayed to buy the next
Sex
Drug
Slandered

Slave
one over one
stuck in slum muck
then hung
on the evening news.
Another one dead.

Do you smell the flies lying undercover?
Sliding sly past the snake's mother,
can you hear the whispers?
Dismiss the real her, 'cause
fake is worth the appeal –
swindled deals.
Pretty faces captured
in a daze.

Tripping in the maze to find the
tilt, notice the sweet smell of rain once
you find your way through the filth.

All of our lives are
distorted to a certain
degree, though the
question is, are you willing
to give into that
distortion? Or will you
break free from the norm
to form your own path?

I believe it's time we all
become Trailblazers!

Morning Thoughts

Growing up is different than I expected. Sure, I have more freedom, but that comes with more responsibilities and casualties of thought – realizing that reality is not what they taught. Following the rules only gets you so far; no one follows rules, they're malleable. Clay visions formed to fractured statues, under false ideals, dangling frivolous fruits – colorful and pungent, but rotten to their roots. Munching minds mold while consuming nature, unwilling to place seeds back on the land they reaped. The earth should be our most important matter since our living, war, peace, dying, buying, greed, crying, laughing, and endearing chaos would not exist without it. No innocence would be lost upon it… which came early for me, but with my ecdysis came an idea. The idea that nothing in this temporary world will bring eternal happiness. Nothing ever remains the same, yet with every pass, stumble, ascension, and fall, the self remains present. The self is key, no matter how battered it may be. You must find peace within. Journey down the trails of your thoughts and find what is important to YOU, because reality is relative. God is just a personification of self. Ponder existence for a moment… Do you hear that inner voice, your voice, the voice only you can hear, a voice that controls decision and debates until all is clear? Divine, is it not?

We've Been Lied To

We've been lied to.
It's in our odd food and
daily programming.
It's intertwined with
the agendas of our
so called 'idols'
dipped in riches, too
stiff to notice or care
about the destruction
they set in motion –
emotions turbulent like
a storm stricken ocean
under our smiling
gray crater moon.

We've been lied to,
you must wake up soon.

History may have brought
us to where we are,
but HIS story is not mine.

Guns are just as precious as diamonds in America,
blood spilled each way
worn on body,
you can't
you won't take away!
Blood Diamonds, gov, and The NRA.
Guns are just as precious as diamonds in
America,
you can't take them away.

RICHES

BLING

Mourning Morning

I see death in the morning
resting along contorted country roads.
I wonder if its passing was instant,
after colliding with sprinting metal.
Did all go black?
Or did it ricochet to the ground and lay
twitching as cool morning air whisked steam
from its fresh flesh wound.

I wonder if it's dark glassy eyes hide a secret observer,
watching clones of the
persecutor drive by without action – indifferent
to the ceremony going on in the woods.

For a moment, I envisioned myself salvaging the horns,
yet that view of self was savage and misused,
compared to the norms of today.
"Not off the side of the road, rotten and dirty,
rather from the forest, with a thirty
and a clean shot to the heart.
Be sure to use every part!"
"But what about the family?"
"What? You mean mine?
Well they'll be well fed and have a pelt for the winter."

Separation.

Out of sight, out of mind – no compassion for those of a
　　different kind.
Selfish.
We encroached on their land.
Imagine if foreign entities imposed their will on YOUR
　　home,
killing your family and changing your way of life.
"Oh, right, like colonization?"

Death due to invasion.

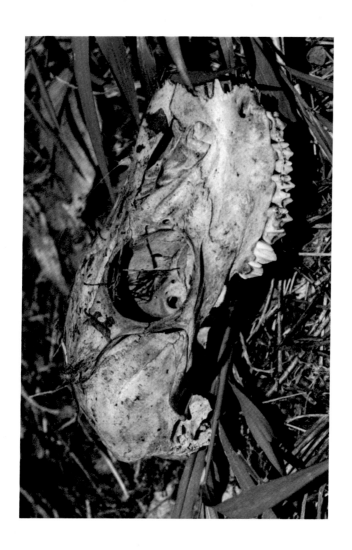

Ignorance was bliss,
but you're no longer a kid.

White Lies

White lies and black ties, let's talk about oppression.
"Here take these pills prescribed for depression,
yet be careful not to abuse them like those rappers do."

"Syrup with no pancakes, Xans when my feelings ache,
Percs cause I'm up too late,
washed down with waves of Ciroc boy!"

Propagated shenanigans
to keep the youth held
down by the Man
again and again.

Fragile ambitions
glisten in the chains that dangle out of foreign cars,
snatching the necks of photoshopped models
while recused voices cry out,

"Scratch my [   ] and I'll help you get ahead.
I've got power you see – stature and authority.
Simply suppress your nasty thoughts of me
and you'll get by."

Mental pressures forced upon us.

Cognitive dissonance
justified by the distance
between ego and self.

Yes, blood diamonds relentlessly
carve neural pathways that
ooze resentment of all kinds – division of aspirations and
     expectations.
No one to trust, nowhere to hide.
You are not yourself.
A ghost in a shell – the omnipresent voice you can't shake,
the parasite taking, to give nothing back.

Whatever happened to a symbiotic relationship?

Ties to chains.
Black meshed with white lifestyles.
The lines are now gray.
"Wealth isn't the same as it was back in the day."

Better infamous than famous.
Notoriously glorious
to no end, sworn by the oath
to uphold the ego at all costs.

White lies may seem harmless now,
but I promise you, they will take on a life of their own.
Like Artificial Intelligence
we won't be able to stop the mayhem unless the plug is
     pulled
… but I'm not sure we know where the outlet is.

One no longer appears as is, in the race
for ornamentation – richness of attire.
Tired avatars and laughter.

Rambling

I don't know what you think
so watch what you speak
when you 'round my street
cause the void ain't filled
where the wild things creep
cause the shit they're feeding
no longer fills our genuine need.

The Black Mirror behind the light
is so good at conditioning,
selling fake dreams
and demanding an offering.

You'll keep coming back,
mentally starving.

So you must meditate
to find your consciousness,
your intuition.
The third eye.

Delve into the mind
to find divine secrets
you never knew
and
stop feeding the rich mimes

stuffed in a room who care not
for the everyday person,
hurting our dreams,
our needs.

The fight for resources
has made us bleed.

No more.
No more.

City Trek

Officers stand by the entrance of the station with large shotguns and gold shells exposed. It's cold. I need a tissue for my nose.

Through the doors, and further down the street, I see a man walking on the sidewalk reading a book. Somehow he plans his steps through the pages – a strange way to get around.

Between sidewalks, I spot a girl with pink pigtails who takes her fluffy earmuffs out of her platinum bag – it must have been a coincidence that I saw her at the same crosswalk hours later. Her hair was down.

Beyond, a vendor sells fruit – some

bruised, some round, like the bodies rushing in every direction. Everyone's lateness is pronounced, profound.

What's left to do but observe when no tech alters your perception? Visual lessons. Without speaking, they call for my attention.

So many scenarios playing out, so many people chasing the fleeting seconds. So many cigarettes and lung clinching smoke, but none for him. Instead, he settles for an old short flattened to the street, near the subway entrance, by a church.

Soon, I find myself behind the jaws of a slick metal serpent, together

we course through time.

Inside a deserted fellow leans and bobs like the half empty can of Monster on the floor. It's ironic that both are usually left on the street, while people ignore and tip-toe over them, as if not to disturb. Yet, upon this underground chariot, a man who spoke a foreign tongue, thought consciously about what he saw... so he picked up the can as he departed. Partial.

During my ascension, two girls thought I didn't see them sneak through the turnstile, but I did, and I'm sure they knew they should have paid, but they were pretty, so they got away with it.

Typical.

Spot any ad in the square of time and you'll see that sex sells – there's nothing like a perfectly sculpted set of cells. I wonder what the creators admire, and I wonder if they intended to have the sugary drink cost less than the fruit juice? I entertain the healthier choice, but my wallet forces me to grab the can full of

hi-fructose.

Typical.

Convo Clay

"Meat, cheese, eggs, and dairy,
I mean c'mon, how many times
are we gonna have this conversation?"
"First we gotta get forty dollars,
or ten fifty."
"One ticket please."
"Nah man, don't worry 'bout me,
we found one on the street, so you can
save that dollar for later, but, do you
know when that comes?"
"Nope, I'm waiting too."

Passing by blank stares
and odd looks; do I know you?
Probably not, but I'd like to, so I'll
fantasize to keep my dreams
satisfied.

On the outside we all seem
fine, even though time jostles us to and fro.
"You can't save everyone, you know."
Voices in the city, conversations to mold.

Highway Woes

Highway veins, littered
with remains of
human consumption,
ooze grimy vibes
of hopelessness,
echoing the thoughts
of those who sit on the cold stone
streets, without a roof.

I want to help,
but I can barely help myself.

I found five dollars yesterday, but I
may need it tomorrow – no time for
charity today.

The world is beautiful,
yet
so much of it needs help,
an insurmountable
task that looms over my consciousness.
A storm cloud over my day.

How can I live comfortably
knowing that so many suffer as
time erodes and Mother Nature

grows ill and old?

So many hearts have grown cold,
desensitized by the violent cries
casted by channels and mediums,
those that alter perception of society and self.

The screens
leech our inhibitions
leaving us numb to the
full vibrations of existence.
A cause bigger than self,
bigger than consumption,
and capitalism.

We are spiritual beings having a human experience.
What we do today creates ripples beyond our existence.

Suburban Wildlife

Suburban wildlife. Quaint, but nothing too wild,
a few plump birds and mangy squirrels
with erratic movements upon a perch.

I assume they're looking for food,
yet the squirrels must not be too hungry
after last night's curb trash,
because they passed by
the fresh shelled walnuts
I tossed outside.

The pedestrians that stroll by
must not abide by the nine to five,
though I can't blame them…
running on their own time and such.

Leisurely going about your day seems so delightful,
full of unexpected trials to keep your attention.
If money was not an issue, this would be every day,
casually observing those who cross my path.

Though I wonder, "What if we are the wild ones,"
stuck in square routines only to ensure
we can maintain the same mundane cycle.

What is keeping us from living comfortably today?

Reveal. Release. Play.
Some of us are a part of suburban wildlife every day,
and society is the speeding car knocking us
to a daze.

College Ruled Napkin

A water stain I had to
mop up

messy things and such
came from my
cool
juice
cup

dead cooked tree
skin neatly lined
blue

cleans up well

swelled with
water
now dirty

bound for a
far off
trash valley

those dirty trash valleys

oh how we can't

seem to control
our steam
and ooze, day
after day…

On one
I hope
to say,

'We can.'

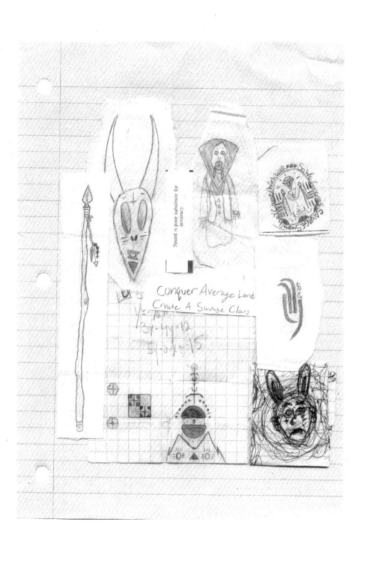

Speed is poor substitute for accuracy.

Conquer Average Land
Create A Savage Clan

The Lost Ones

It's the beginning of an end,
humanity's own demise.
On false surfaces we depend,
leaving our truths to rot and lie.

Nature has been pushed to its boundaries,
allowing the concrete jungle to flourish.
The invaluable devices and their batteries
may be the reason we all perish.

We were once in tune with our higher selves,
the mind and senses in flow with the cosmic swing,
but now the screens approve our feelings,
ears keen to the sound of a ring.

Are we the drones we feared would take over?

'Disaster lurks 'round our precious findings,
'cause luck can be drained from a clover.'

Black holes behind the black mirror…
Falling.
Time lost through a screen
a lost structure
a torn seam.

Dreams of tipping the
crown off the master,
a grand disaster.

Ashes and rubble
we must battle
we must rebuild…
rebuild the lost ones.

Red Lights and Thumb Swipes

Red lights and thumb swipes,
are you even paying attention?

I see faults in the reflections of my mirrors
and cheap tinted windows.
Others' inability to focus on one thing,
an important thing,
a heavy metal dangerous thing.

You would think the darkness between
blinks would be enough, but no,
we need more distractions. 'Make it tough!'
"How about I use one hand to steer and veer
my view off to the glistening screen in my other hand,
and I'll hunt for letters too – weaving semi-cohesive
      sentences
of half-words and acronyms that likely lack importance.
Though don't worry,
I'll be safe, foot always ready to punch the brake."

But wait…
let's think about this for a second,
as if the issue is a microcosm of society today:
Focus, we lack it.
Stimulation has become shorter
and we long for its shortness,

thinking we're getting information in tight bits – swipe,
    switch, on to the next clip.
"If it's going to keep my attention, then it better be THE
    BEST."
… but it lacks substance and so do we.

So I ask: if we expect so little from what we receive,
then what will become of our speech, our relationships
and how we treat those on the street?

Long form discourse is **dead**
and critical thinking is holding on by a thread.
If we surrender our attention and questions to the almighty
    devices,
then they will become the ones in charge of our vices –
dangling and tangling the puppet strings that make us
    dance
entranced by the hidden algorithms that show
only a piece of the puzzle.
While the full image remains muzzled and trapped
behind a high-voltage barbed wire cage.

We are in the age of knowing,
though we have forgotten how much we still must learn.

Red lights and thumb swipes.
Are you even paying attention?

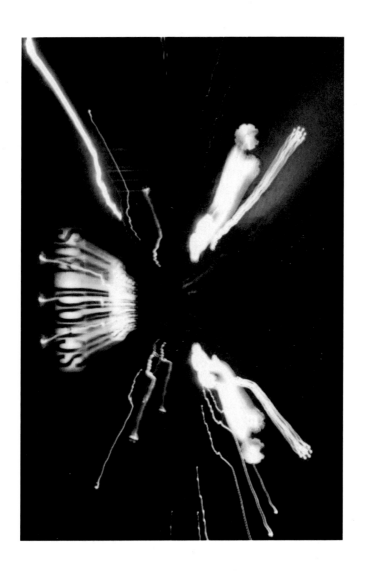

Smashed Soap

Smashed soap and dirty dreams
leave no hope for the soul stuck
in an endless scheme,
and no solace for the jealous man,
for the shield of one's ego feuds all knowledge.

It's hard to walk away
in this modern world, where every man and woman
battles for their talent to be in the forefront.
It's hard to put down the buzzing screen
teeming with updates – the newest gilded cage to seal our
       fate.

Though no one knows what the future holds,
it could all end tomorrow…
for the sun owes us no mercy in its gravitational dance.
A waltz among the stars, while on earth we remain in a
       trance.
A cycle fueled by our trivialities,
department stores going out of business
because they were endlessly stuffed with
our wants rather than our needs.
'Pillage the land, kill their culture, and cut the trees.'
And they're stuck wondering why it's hard to breathe?

Well I'll tell ya' why, driven by your carelessness

you feel that you are above others,
when in reality we are all grounded,
shrouded in a monetary divide that we created while
idolizing the rich, who are great at playing pretend
or can really send a ball in that big-boy playground game.
From beginning to end, we rarely change.

Primal,
jostling to be the apex.
In denial, because we believe that the
next will be the best,
but on edge, because the
next is always met by the next
claiming to be better than the best.

Dirty deeds weave the noose
around the neck of our hopes and dreams.

Even the soap you use to get clean
won't gleam in face of judgement.
Themis laughed in my face
when I told her we discovered the summit.

Digital Dissent

We want to be extra.
We want to be liked.
We want to be loved,
but no one wants to give up the front.

'All hail the luminous avatars.'

Lost in a forest of fiber optics,
sick of swallowing plastic.

"You're destroying me, you know?
And I hate you for that.
I hate your lies,
and how you built me up
just so you could
swing your wrecking ball
through my heart."

His bloody bone scaffolding
crumbled, as she fell apart.

"Now I'm a ruin,
a ghost,
and I hate the world
just a little bit more
than yesterday."

Holographic Drip

Holographic living
leads empty repetition
leaving leaky feelings
dripping down the walls
of my self-will.
Selfishly
I will drown in the depths
of my wants
ignoring my needs until I
decompose and bleed,
soaking through to the next floor.
Creaky floorboards bored of my
petulant pacing,
mind racing
as I try to put something together
that makes… sense.

Please Don't Believe Me

No,
I do not project reality.
See, everything you see in me is produced,
like that food on your plate – manufactured to a certain
      taste.
How do your eyes feel?
Are they drooling yet?
I mean these trivialities I'm dishing out
are downright delicious.

Superficial dreams to craft white noise sheep.

Yes, yes!
Gather with the herd and wait to be harvested and cloned.
'You've become perfect little drones.'

There's no magic in the real world,
You'll find everything you need in me.
I mean sure,
it'll be stripped of any true meaning and shadowed by
      one's agenda,
but your distracted mind will accept all as "just fine".

WE ARE WATCHING YOU!

Yes, Big Brother has been here for a while,
and you've been steeping in his gaze – how does it taste?
The true American pie:
manufactured dreams and hollow lives!

Sincerely,
TV

Let Go

Distractions
to lose traction,
we've forgotten how to let go
let go
let go.
Let's go to that place we used to know.

That cove in the forest where the sun
broke through the trees,
and the breeze tickled your knees
as we laid bare across the leaves.

I want to be primal again.
I'm tired of luxuries
I'm tired of technology
I don't want to be connected
I want my privacy back
No more passwords
No more trends
No more!

Just leave!
Roam to the
farthest shore,
where land
claims no warmth.

Then
peer off the edge,
but don't think twice,
the fall will steer you right.
The fall
The fall
F
A
L
L
Are you all right?
I bet you can really feel it now,
you know, life.
The feeling of Prana coursing
through your fleshy veins.
Let go, just let go of the frame.

Nimbus Cloud

I long for sleep, but linger in between,
choking on the smoke from a pipe dream.

Pillow hard,
no feathers
just rubble and shards.
A burst bubble,
damn…
reality hits hard
when you're swimming in lofty thoughts.

Head in the clouds, forgetting what I was taught.

Lost,
finding an ease of mind while
caught in the infinite moment
as the momentum of molecules soothe the flow
of energy that wax and wane through my psyche.

Above it all, I can finally see.

Energetic Waves

Waves of melancholy crash against
battered shores.

In the sand,
I lay still as coarse fragments
of sea stones
and shells irritate my fragile body.

I can't help but imagine the worst,
since the best of my thoughts
rarely reach fruition
frustrated because it feels like
there's something missing,
but there isn't.

I am all I can be in this
infinite moment,
finite to an extent,
but measured by us
it never ends

changing
frequency,
color,
shape,
and size.

Energy transferred from me to you

... can you feel it?

The Place She Left

I'm looking for a place,
though I'm not quite sure
how to get there
or if it exists,
but I have a feeling,
a strong feeling it does.
Like goosebumps crawling
down
my spine
as the pressure of time
squeezes my chest
and contorts my mind.

Circus thoughts
performing under a big top
leaping through rings of flames,
so high up, but it's all an act – a precise
distraction from what is real.

Action to foot the bill as
distressed squeals
peel back the layers of
what you thought was real.

She scalped your desires,
your idols,

and now you're
left wondering,
"Does this place even exist?"

I want to escape
and never look back,
but invisible anchors
scrape the sea floor of my notions.

Tension waves crashing
from the blood red ocean.

Are you floating?

My lungs turn to pitchers,
but I'm not thirsty
and the water is murky.

Shadows lurk
beneath below…

"Is this place even real?"

Numb
as hungry woes whisk
a stench so rotten:

my decaying love.

Emotional Con

Emoticons.

False idols,
an emotional con.

The heart sent
was not yours – stone faced
"lol",
no words.

We've abbreviated our lives
and there's
no turning back.

I know you're
filled with anxiety when you
don't get a text back.

Read.
Ellipses…
but no response.

Device tossed,
screen cracked.

Swiping across

fissures as fingers
bleed a black mixture
of dripping
LCD liquid
sipped to
blend into the matrix
where frayed fiber optics
connect to send
minds to the fray of silicon
and microchips.

The hand in bag
dips below the void.

So much static,
too much noise.

A Sip of Love

Touch,
a feeling so deep.
Deep,
a void I'll fall to with ease.
A tease,
the heat of your aura
tingles my senses – defenseless.
I surrender to you
senseless in the daze they call love,
but love is just a feeling and feelings often
dwindle and views often swivel
because life is trapped in constant motion.
To live is a spell...
Our breath, this feeling – our potion.

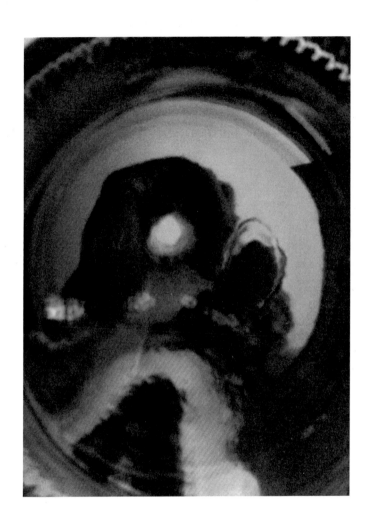

Blame?

Desires crushed under the rubble of faded dreams.
Why put so much trust in someone you don't know?

Digital facades weaving fanciful tales so distant from
　　reality.
Is anything true any more?

This pain is worse than physical,
a glitch in the psyche.
It lingers, it stings, and the taste is so damn bitter.

I thought of you as I fell asleep,
but you were nothing more
than a brief distraction.
I wish that wasn't true,
but I can't blame you.
I blame myself.

I blame myself for falling for your words,
your compliments, your aesthetic.

We took the world in my dreams last night,
we were unstoppable…
but the more I think about it,
the more I fear my vulnerability – inclined to
let my thoughts roam wild and free.
I'm alone, but I'm not lonely, or

maybe I am.

No, you can't blame me for wanting to love again.

Encountering the Same

The spontaneous encounters
that allude to fate,
negate the fading
illusions in my mind.

Divine duality at its best.

I crave consistency,
but hate repetition,
inner self not willing to listen
petitioning to run away from
the humdrum monotonous
slums of societal living:

wake, work, eat, sleep
repeat
repeat.
So often that I have
memorized the morning traffic
pattern – pathetic, yet
apathetic to the eclectic side
of I, making something out of
nothing.

A wheel.
A lie.

A cup full of
mystifying drool
dripped from the sandman's
lips
lapped to take a trip
down the path of the
Panther's Shadow.

Volatile views from the daydream pew,
praying to the voice behind thought.
"I'm listening, I'm here."
… spontaneous encounters with my truest self,
who has arrived with open ears.

Too Good

Good music and good conversation,
two things that could save this nation,
though the disconnect between locations
has me shuffling disbelief.
Lies intertwined in lines we can't leave,
while sun scorched seeds, standing in
the lost forest, fall to their knees.
Sorry for my rambling, but I'm trying my best,
a poem just for you sparked by the
few words beneath your quiet smile.
A beautiful smile,
one that alludes to more than a screen can convey.
Beyond what my screen displays,
I'd love to delve into your desires and explore your
creativity.
Red roses dance in shadows of leaves,
while drawn hearts bleed dreams of euphoria.
Anything is possible on earth,
and I'd love to explore it with ya.

Crooked Crown

It's quiet behind the mote.

I often hate the
sound of silence.

In it, thoughts become violent,
past, present, and future
collide,
causing my inner demons
to whine and howl.

My tongue aches from all the twisted
lies – stories contrived just so I can get
by, bye.
Bye
to my old self.

I'm not sure I know
who you are any more.

A crooked crown reflected in the
mirror, across the moor
… Bang!

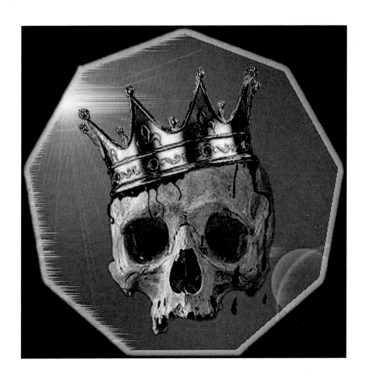

We Own the Night

Once they fall asleep and the roads grow silent,
we roam along the shadows drifting – defiant.
Wild and Free we see through your hollow lies
slipping through spires of time… Eternal,
searching for the internal meaning of life's bliss,
whilst tasting the colors of the wind – nature's kiss.

WE OWN THE NIGHT!

Identity

Believe in one's
identity,
as one knows

the tide will return
accordingly and in
the end

die with peace as
the net is dyed
red; a floating

piece wading
while they dine by
candle light, to talk
about their vices

eating the good
to maintain a
proper diet.

Be quiet when
you creep with them
into the den,

because one wrong

cross may lead
to your end.

Ten small
soldiers stand
ready by the tent.

Savage,
but the same
in their intent,

ready to tie down
the deity they thought
to be true,

forcing a dent
between dimensions.

'We can cross back and forth,
write our own course,
revealing mysteries
so golden, so true.'

We are the gods
of our own existence,
floating entities
lost in the distance.

Dig Deep

While dancing with Lila in duality
I sift through the lingering bliss of my childhood grit,
forest trails and Saturday morning cartoons,
what a trip.

Pinky and the Brain schemes on screens
trying to gain a vice grip on the world
and many things,
man-made things
and dreams – gleaming busted silly things.
A false facade catering to those
who hum and nod
to the tune of odd lies
and woeful cries.

They've forgot the forgotten.

Ancient civilizations
treated like fruit that was rotten,
yet their seeds were divine,
waiting for spring to blossom
and meet their kin.

I often dream about running
away to the forest,
back to meet him…
my past self.

The one with the body that
dealt with our infant wishes
of infinite wishes
and golden dishes
filled with fruitful bounty.
Dining at the table with our council
we dealt with those who praised
almighty hopeless ideologies.

I cannot see
I will not see
for this is not my home
not my home
not my home
a nomad

near and far
forever
I shall roam
I shall roam
inside my mind
and through the dirt
into love
I'm sure we'll hurt
but in that pain
I'll find a meaning
a reason
and above it all
a higher being.

The Rabbit

Through the tunnel,
to the other side,
I crawled
to survive.
I crawled
through your web of lies,
the ones spun by the
crimes of forgotten lives.
Please,
send help... please we need help!
No not them, but me,
because my two selves have now split to three.
Yes, a trinity of desires – forbidden so I must not speak...
There are dreams to chase and tea to taste.
No time for sleep.

Sorcerer Begs

"… if you let me in,
I swear I won't let you down.
I swear I won't disappoint you.
You won't have to cash in your poison possessions,
because the baggage I carry is priceless:
scars that tell endless tales
and trinkets from divine destinations.
Soon enough I'll become the hero of your daydreams,
but first you'll have to let me in."

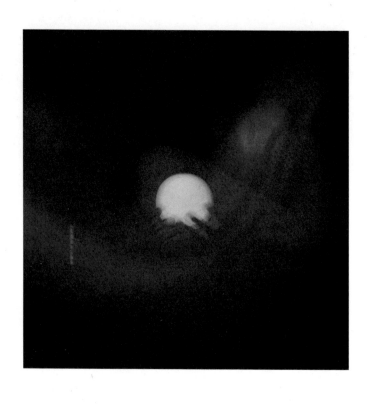

Untitled Five

I want to know I'm alive, and that one day I
will be remembered. Not by one, but
everyone. I-I'm not selfish... well, I'm less
than most, but I mean if you're not looking
out for yourself then you're bound to grind
gears eventually; that's friction, right?
I don't even know what "this" is, do you?
Did the pendulum swing when she flew
through her dreams, past crystal streams
by dragonflies, folly, and flowers? I think a
dead rose is prettier than a live one, but I
guess it's missing its scent. Cent. Sent away
to another place, where inhibitions are low
and expectations are high, your blood
rushes fast and you feel alive and I feel alive.
Can you feel it in your chest? Yes, right there
in the center. What a peaceful spinning orb.
I-I always feel hot. Red hot, hands hot, feet
hot, body flush with feeling. I can fog a cold
piece of glass without touching it; energy I
can't control. Ugh, I'm working on it though,
like them railroads... yeah, building a trail to
infinity where I'll dance with Persephone to
the beat of blooming flowers, and the
Harbinger will tell Hades how much She
really hated him, ya'know, P... Anyway, I've

heard the bump that goes in the night; it growls and grumbles like a wild warthog prodding its territory, but that's part of another story.

Forgotten Unity

The locks on my head
remind me that "time"
continues to pass.

Though time is nothing
more than a man-made
measure to see how long
this will last.

Kindred souls from above
locked in fragile flesh avatars.

Gods with amnesia.

We've come so far,
but the daily squabbles
threaten our good will.

Only once we relinquish
our need to be right and
adopt the notion of
absolute truth, will we be
able to find bliss in the dirt
and connectivity in our roots.

XXXVII

Omoimasu

We are gods with amnesia,
eternal spirits
temporary humans.
Our lives are not the beginning,
nor the end, but
simply a rest stop on an endless journey.
Yes, through the universe and beyond.
Sci-fi?
No, more like Wi-Fi,
a seamless connection between
every human, animal, and plant.
We are not separate from the earth,
and the earth is not separate from the universe.

All is one.

Spiraling clusters from a single **BANG**
comprised of
gas and dust and
sacred minerals,
compressed to orbiting planets
that mimic the dance of our atoms.

The veins of a river, to the veins of a leaf,
to the highway veins that connect our streets,
not far from the veins that pump blood beneath our skin.

As above, so below.

Though, worries of succumbing to a blackhole
where no light
no sound
where nothing grows.

Fear of the unknown.

There's more to the story,
something doesn't add up.

Are we creating the math to understand
this world, or we discovering what was left for us?
If so, then we have more to discuss.

Untitled Six

Stones and sticks break brittle bones, it's
too hot to stay in our home. My chapstick is
melt to shit and I've had just about enough
of this strange weather, but whatever,
there's only so much that we can control:
like what we eat, what we pay attention to,
who we vote for, etc, etc. Extra this, too
much that, spending life collecting things,
only to throw them away on a day when you
find them, dusty and forgotten, stacked and
wedged into some spider infested corner in
the attic that sags, bringing down the
property value – too specific? Oh well, it's
all in the details. Spiny tales wrapped
'round my two feet. "Where are you
dragging me?"

"Don't be afraid."

Well... okay... that's easy for you to say when
You're sitting comfy in the observatory,
desensitized by your lack of compassion.
Are you fake laughing? People dragging
their feet in complacency irritates me
to the point of no return – emotions
churned like thick magma
oozing from an angry volcano.

"Is this what hell feels like? The pressure of becoming a lost memory heated by the guilt of not doing what you wanted, forced to relive the same pathetic moment over, and over, and over, and over again."
… but I digress.

Sea Salt Wounds

We swam in an ocean
full of hope – it ran deep.

The sun glistened
through the crystal current
causing a lapse of reality as
waves of tranquility washed
lackadaisical seaweed upon
my knees – at ease, coasting
along ocean breeze.

You convinced me to dive,
so without hesitation we
became one with the weight of
the water.

We saw shipwrecked martyrs and
coral structures, rife with psychedelic
fish whispering secrets into ascending
bubbles.

We sank deeper.

The pressure was immense and the
tense of time dissolved,
along with my breath.

It was dark and my bones chilled,
but you said I'd be all right.

Amidst the darkness,
bioluminescent algae
compelled the deep waves
to mimic the night sky.

As above, so below.

Forced to behold,
I felt numb.

"Please, one last kiss,
before we're done."

In the Sound of Silence

Have you ever heard
the sound of silence?

Like the cold 'crete in
the basement of an
abandoned lodge,

or high upon a mountain top.

Among the silence…

a hum.

An echo
echoing in the distance.

The buzz of the world I suppose.

Creatures mingling
in a shared existence.

The sky cradles us
while the universe
strangles the earth,
suffocating it
by the sand sieved

through the hands of
Father Time.

Sometimes I think
the design of the world is
mine,

and sometimes
I feel like an avatar
with a task assigned,

but among the
silence I find life
redefined.

Alike

Shrines of divine beings
bind far out meanings
to the life
we call reality.

But what is real?
Is it what you feel,
hear,
see,
or touch?

Because the spirits that roam
the empty halls of my temple
whisper secrets of
much

more.

Concepts beyond
the understanding of
what's
good or bad.

Man-made plans,
projections of us on them…

a way to make sense
of the madness.

You can't have one without the other,
so it's safe to say we will always
agree to disagree,
but believe me
we can reach a point of peace
acknowledging that
we all hurt,
we all laugh,
we all cry,
we all dream,
and we all die.

We are more alike than they divide.

Peaking

Ask nothing of the past,
but give thanks to the passed time
that allows you to shine in this moment,
the infinite moment.
Finite when the light is found glistening
by the edge of the well – fears quelled,
leveled to a state of being where all is well.
'But what if this is all an illusion?'
Then there is more to life than we've been assuming.
Amusing.
Notions of diving into the rabbit hole to find Alice.
Kaleidoscope eyes wide, peeking through the lattice.

Reset

Invincible

Insufferable in the presence of outside advice – unwilling
    to inherit thoughts beyond the "made-up" mind.

Nostalgic towards former accomplishments, those that
    were wicked and frowned
    upon, but so thrilling in the moment.

Vices, deemed as fuel – fuel for a fast life.

Inside we are broken, but on the outside you won't see a
    scratch.

No regrets, until confronted by reality, and yet we still
    waver on,

Concerned with nothing but the "come up". The rise to be
    the best, arrogant with every step.

Indecisively between thoughts to the point where reality is
    blurred – a place
    where actions have no consequence,

Blaming cross outcomes on everyone but yourself.

Lies become truth, engrained in every wrong action, every
    word, and every thought.

Educing demons into the real world in a dangerous dance
    with the devil. I used to think I was Invincible, but I
    am not, none of us are.

The Fast Life

Will chew you up and spit you out,
fueled by suppressed demons and false ideals –
chasing hollow idols through veiled screens.
'Do it for the money, sign with the devil and your soul
will earn plenty,' but it's
dark where the grass is greener – quite lonely behind
castle walls, where the weary ruler submits to
seclusion in fear of being prosecuted by those he
harmed. Chasing the fast life will chew you up and
spit you out.
It happened to Mac, Avicii, Peep, Juice and Yams.
Just ask the twenty-seven club. Ask
them how cruel the unforgiving substances were. Ask
them how their creativity was strained by the lime-
light, chasing fans and recognition to become a living
legend… but now they are martyrs – solemn
reminders of how fragile our flesh capsules are.
Cherish what you have now,
because in pursuit of the fast life, there is no winning.

He Unintentionally Flew Through the Sky...

"I whipped around the corner with a speed that made
   reality blur, a speed that
tossed me into a new timeline – the transition was harsh,
   but necessary."

"You were on your way to **Hell** young man, a place I know
   you've seen in your
dreams, a place where nothing right cuts between your
   seams – the ones that
hold your body together. Ask yourself, do you love you?
   Look deep into the
timeless mirror, the one with scrapes and splotches, and
   ask yourself those
questions that scare you the most. What does the future
   hold? Who are you?
What do you stand for and why?
Maybe then you'll know why the universe did not let you
   die."

He found his reset button in the dark,
a new beginning
an opportunity to restart.

Fool's Gold

Stuck.
Obligations tethering self to unwanted situations,
like a hungry fish to a drifting hook
pulled through rough current
tearing iridescent scales to dull remnants
of what used to be,
starry-eyed among an open sea,
but now you have nowhere to go.
Strangled by a net thrown
now clustered in a muck of mundane.
Looking around it seems
we're all stuck in the same
situation.
Hope and happiness dwindle to frustration.
Repeating repetition
sounds so redundant, but this cycle
leaves me no choice, skipping
like a scratched CD in a Sony
Walkman strapped to me as I sink deep
into a pool of quicksand steeping with
deceit.
Why did you lie to me?
You said I'd find my way if I followed
your path, yet the final destination appears
further with every step,
a funhouse I never
agreed to enter, yet my reflection in the room of
mirrors says otherwise – one laughs, while the other cries,
Melpomene and Thalia, perfect pretenders.

Raid the Citadel

As we lay siege to the citadel,
all hell breaks loose,
the cogs fly off their spindles,
the desperate try to swindle, and
families flee and grab anything that will make the enemy
Bleed.
Bleed.
Bleed.

Death comes in threes.

Flames reach their top degree,
melting metals and scorching knees.
There's no one left to bow to.

No one left to ask about you,
or tell your story.
Laugh now,
love now,
fight now,
for this may be the last time you get a chance.

Doomed to be among the patterned corpses,
bound to be in a trance.
Lost in a drone-like state,
full of sorrow and hate

strained to your limit with no energy to debate.
But there is still time to change your path.

Bleed.
Bleed.
Bleed.

Death comes in threes.

What will you do when the dying system
knocks you to your knees?

Have You Ever

Have you ever felt like you don't belong, like the life
 you're living is not yours?
Have you ever felt like no one is listening?
Have you ever lost hope?
Have you been labeled weird, strange, or an outcast?
Do you feel lost at times?
Do you feel connected to the universe?
Do you enjoy uplifting the lives of those around you, with
 compassion?
Do you feel connected to a cause greater than yourself?
Can you feel the subtle energies in the room?
Can you sense the disconnect between modern generations
 and nature?
Can you view situations objectively?
Have you ever dreamed a dream so grand that it gave you
 chills?
Have you had enough of the bullshit and lies propagated
 by the mainstream media
and politics?
Are you ready to stand up to those who attack the peace
 and free will, that EVERY human on earth deserves?
… If so, you are not alone.
I cannot promise you I will change everything, but I can
 promise that I will devote part of my existence to
 mending the divide that quakes in our country, and
 this world.

Their greedy agendas must come to an end, and for that to happen we must band together, and accept our differences.

It is time to take back what is rightfully ours!

This is only the beginning.

There is no limit to knowing. Anyone who claims to know it all, is lying. Though, every day lends an opportunity to discover something new, about yourself or the world; magic is real and it's all around us.

About the Author

E.G. Chambers was raised in the suburban area of Philadelphia, Pennsylvania. At a young age, he showed an affinity for adventure and storytelling. Long hikes in the woods with his brother, never ending bike rides, and hours of outside play, became fuel for his imagination.

Once E.G. learned how to craft stories from his adventures, he saw no limit to the possibilities of how he shared his thoughts and ideas about the world. He found that he could expand his reality and relive those adventures through the magic of words, and thus, his inner storyteller was born. E.G. shared these tales with family and friends, and to his delight they were interested. The expressions, smiles, and laughter he received, fueled his search for more experiences to share. But it wasn't until an eighth grade English class that E.G. was introduced to poetry. He learned that he did not have to write an entire story to create rich characters, with expansive landscapes. Through poetry, he could invite readers into a whole new world, with a few carefully crafted stanzas.

In 2017 E.G. received his bachelor's degree in Communications, with a minor in social media marketing, from St. Thomas Aquinas College in Sparkill, New York. Having studied the things he loved, at a higher level, E.G. felt a new appreciation for the media that keeps us entertained. He learned that all forms of media have one thing in common…writing. This new found knowledge was held close to his heart. E.G. then began cataloging every liberating thought and moment of importance in the form of a photograph or a poem.

E.G. appreciates the freedom and intimacy that poetry lends to its authors and audience. He enjoys bending the rules of grammar and the English language. Poetry is his safe space, a place where he can peacefully explore his reality. The revelation that he is not alone in his notions of life, culminated in the creation of this book:

"With poetry as my vehicle, I cruise down the backroads of the existential, among the mountains of the metaphysical where I find myself on the edge of what I perceive to be true. In that space, sprouts the gift of words I share with you, my kindred souls. You reflect a part of me and I hope you find solace among these pages."